Samuel Francis Creswell

Collections Towards the History of Printing in

Nottinghamshire

With an index of persons and subjects

Samuel Francis Creswell

Collections Towards the History of Printing in Nottinghamshire
With an index of persons and subjects

ISBN/EAN: 9783337251338

Printed in Europe, USA, Canada, Australia, Japan

Cover: Foto ©ninafisch / pixelio.de

More available books at **www.hansebooks.com**

COLLECTIONS

TOWARDS THE

HISTORY OF PRINTING

IN

NOTTINGHAMSHIRE.

BY THE

REV. S. F. CRESWELL, M.A., F.R.G.S., F.R.A.S.,

LATE SCHOLAR OF ST. JOHN'S COLLEGE, CAMBRIDGE.

LONDON:

JOHN RUSSELL SMITH,

36, SOHO SQUARE.

M.DCCC.LXIII.

LOCAL TYPOGRAPHY.

WHEN we consider the distance which once virtually sepa-
rated the provinces from London, it will appear likely that
many strange pieces by well-known hands, many curious
editions, and much evidence respecting local interests, remain
to be discovered. As soon as the materials throughout the
country shall have become sufficient, the general enquirer,
(perhaps another Buckle,) will be able to pick out facts and
draw conclusions as to the current of thought, wealth, and
enterprise, through the country: from the fluctuations in
quality, quantity, and kind of subject matter; from the epoch
and duration of provincial discussions, from the parties to
them, and the grounds they adopted; from comparison of the
dates of local printing, from the style of typography, from
reprints, and the connections between Town and Country
booksellers. In this general enquiry, antiquarians must pro-

vide for the historian by gathering local evidence; hence the following Collections.

This tract contains an experimental catalogue of books, pamphlets, and single sheets, printed and published in Nottingham only; I hope to be able to give at some future time a similar list for the other towns in the County, as well as an account of the newspapers.

My acknowledgements are due to the late Mr. Thomas Bateman, F.S.A., and to Messrs. Llewellynn Jewitt, F.S.A., R. Preston and H. Jackson.

Any note, addition, correction, or suggestion—also offers of sale, exchange, or loan—will be received with thanks.

The vols. merely *published* in Nottingham are marked thus *.

S. F. CRESWELL.

THE CATHEDRAL SCHOOL, DURHAM.

TYPOGRAPHY OF NOTTINGHAMSHIRE.

NOTTINGHAM.

PART I.—BOOKS, PAMPHLETS, AND SINGLE SHEETS.

NOTE.—*Deering, in his 'Nottinghamia Vetus et Nova,' gives the number of Booksellers as two, of Printers as one, in 1641, which had increased to three and two respectively, in 1739.*

* The Being and Well-Being of a Christian. In Three Treatises : The First, Setting forth the Properties of the Righteous. The Second, The Excellency of Grace. The Third, The Nature and Sweetness of Fellowship with Christ. By Edward Reyner, late Minister of the Gospel in Lincoln. Together with an INTRODUCTORY DISCOURSE, containing Mens mistakes about Grace, and their Chief Happiness, and the true Nature of both ; with a Character of a Gracious Person, and the great Absurdity of those Cavils and Reproaches he meets with from the World. By the *PUBLISHER*, J. Reyner. London, Printed, by R. W. for Henry Mortlock, at the Sign of the White Hart in Westminster-Hall : and Samuel Richards Bookseller in Nottingham, 1669. (small oct., pp. 390.)

' John Dunton mentions a Mr. Richards, bookseller, of Nottingham, of whom he says, he " Pursues his business very closely, and is a person of great integrity. I dwelt with him two years, and found him a good paymaster." '—TIMPERLEY.

* GOOD WILL TOWARDS MEN, OR A TREATISE OF THE COVENANTS, Viz. Of *WORKS* and Of *GRACE* OLD & NEW. Wherein sundry *Propositions* are Laid down Concerning them, and Diverse *Questions* occasionally Discussed. By a Lover of Truth and Peace. *LONDON*, Printed, for Samuel Richards, Book-seller in Nottingham, 1675. (sm. oct. 494, + The Table, pp. 7. Author the Rev. John Barrett, M.A., of St. Peter's, Nottingham, who was ejected 1662, and died Oct. 30, 1713, aged 82 years.)

* THE Christian Temper: OR, A DISCOURSE concerning the Nature and Properties of the Graces of *Sanctification.* Written for Help in *Self-Examination* and *Holy Living.* By JOHN BARRET, M.A. *LONDON*, Printed for *Jonathan Robinson* at the Golden Lion in St. *Pauls* Church-yard, and *Samuel Richards* Bookseller in *Nottingham.* 1678. (small oct., pp. 223.)

* A SERMON Preached before the JUDGE AT THE ASSIZES Held at NOTTINGHAM, On the 19*th* of *July,* 1689. By *W. WILSON,* M.A. Rector of St. *Peter's* Church in *Nottingham. LONDON*, Printed for *Awnsham Churchill* at the Black Swan at *Amen-Corner,* and are to be sold by *Joseph Howe,* Bookseller in *Nottingham,* MDCLXXXIX. (square oct., pp. 31.)

* A SERMON Preached at the CHURCH OF St. *Mary* in *Nottingham:* TO THE SOCIETY FOR *Reformation of Manners.* On *July* the 6th. being the usual Lecture-Day. By *DANIEL CHADWICK* Vicar of *Arnhall,* and one of the Lecturers there. Malachy 3. 16. *Then they that feared the Lord, spake often one to another. London:* Printed for *John Richards* Bookseller in *Nottingham,* 1698. (16mo., pp. 56.)

* THAT 𝕲𝖗𝖊𝖆𝖙 𝕯𝖚𝖙𝖞, AND Comfortable Evidence [*Keeping our selves from our iniquity.*] Opened and applied in some SERMONS upon *Psal.* 18. 23. By *John Whitlock* Minister of the Gospel in *Nottingham. LONDON*, Printed for *Thomas Parkhurst,* and are to be sold by *John Richards* Bookseller at *Nottingham.* 1698. (16mo., pp. 116.)

* THE REMAINS OF Mr. *Joseph Barrett* Son of the Reverend Mr. *John Barrett* Minister of the Gospel AT NOTTINGHAM.

BEING The Second PART taken out of an Exact DIARY written by his own Hand. London: *PRINTED* for *Tho. Parkhurst*, and are to be Sold by him at the *Bible* and *Three Crowns* in *Cheapside*, and *John Richards* at *Nottingham.* 1700. (small oct., pp. 216.)

* A SERMON Preach'd before the Right Worshipful the MAYOR and CORPORATION Of the Town and County of NOTTING-HAM, IN THE Parish Church of St. *MARY* In the said Town, *December* 3. 1702. BEING THE DAY of THANKSGIVING FOR THE Signal Successes GOD has been pleased to grant to Her MAJESTIES Forces both by SEA and LAND. By *EDWARD CLARKE*, M.A. and Vicar there. 𝔓𝔲𝔟𝔩𝔦𝔰𝔥'𝔡 𝔞𝔱 𝔱𝔥𝔢 ℜ𝔢𝔮𝔲𝔢𝔰𝔱 𝔬𝔣 𝔱𝔥𝔢 𝔄𝔲𝔡𝔦𝔢𝔫𝔠𝔢. *London*, Printed for *Edw. Evets*, at the *Green Dragon* in St. *Paul's* Church-yard, and *Gervas Sulley*, Bookseller in *Nottingham.* 1703. (square oct., pp. 4 of Title and Epistle Dedicatory, + pp. 28.)

* A DISCOURSE CONCERNING Pardon of Sin, AND THE BLESSEDNESS OF A *Pardon'd State.* By *John Barrett*, M.A. Minister of the Gospel in *Nottingham. LONDON:* Printed for *J. Robinson*, at the *Golden Lion* in St. *Paul's* Church-yard; and Sold by *Hannah Richards*, in *Nottingham*, 1703. (24mo. pp. 8, consisting of title, preface and advertisement, + pp. 184.)

* A SERMON Preach'd at *S^t. Mary's Nottingham*, On *Friday* the 28th of *July* 1710. Before the HONOURABLE Sir *Littleton Powys*, AND Sir *Salathiel Lovel*, Knights, Her MAJESTY's Justices of Assize for the County of *Nottingham*, &c. By *SAMUEL BERDMORE*, M.A. Vicar of St. *Mary's Nottingham. Publish'd at the Request of the High-Sheriff and the Gentlemen of the Grand-Jury. LONDON*, Printed for *Will. Ward*, Bookseller in *Nottingham:* And Sold by *James Knapton*, at the *Crown* in St. *Paul's* Church-Yard. 1710. (sq. oct., pp. 4 of title and dedication, + pp. 22.)

* *Zeal for the Duty's of the* Christian Religion *as Establish'd in the* Church *of* England; *in opposition, both to the Additions of the* Church *of* Rome, *and the Prejudice of our Dissenters.* A SERMON

PREACH'D at the ASSIZES Held at *NOTTINGHAM.* On *Friday* the 24th of *July*, 1713. Before the Right Honourable the Lord Chief Justice *TREVOR*, And the Honourable Mr. Baron *PRICE.* By *ROBERT MARSDEN*, B.D. Rector of *Rempston*, and late Fellow of *Jesus* Colledge in *Cambridge. Published at the Request of the* HIGH SHERIFF, *and the* Gentlemen *of the* GRAND JURY. *LONDON*, Printed for *W. Ward* Bookseller in *Nottingham*, and *Tho. Varnam* and *J. Osborn*, at the *Oxford-Arms* in *Lombard-street.* 1713. (oct. pp. 30.)

> In Nichols's Lit. An., I. 142, under the year 1717, mention is made of "Remarks on the Bishop of Bangor's Sermon, by Robert Marsden, B.D.;" second edition; and in the note, the author is mentioned as 'Of Jesus college, Cambridge, B.A. 1687; M.A. 1691; B.D. 1700. He was archdeacon of Nottingham, and prebendary of Southwell; and dying in August 1748, at the advanced age of 90, was buried in Rempston church-yard. He published a Concio ad Clerum 1701; an Assize-Sermon 1713; and a Funeral Sermon 1729.' Also on page 511, speaking of Peck, 'He was editor in 1739, of "Nineteen Letters of the reverend and truly learned Henry Hammond, D.D. (Author of the Annotations on the New Testament, &c.) written to Mr. Peter Stainnough and Dr. Nathanael Angelo, many of them on curious subjects, &c. These were printed from the originals, communicated by Mr. Robert Marsden, archdeacon of Nottingham, and Mr. John Worthington.'

Christianity indeed; OR, The Well-disciplin'd CHRISTIAN THE Delight of Christ. SHEWING, How Believers in Christ ought to go in and out each before other in Gospel-Order; Governing, and being Governed, as the Children of one Father. *The Second Edition.* By *FR. STANLEY.* Phil. 4. 8. *Finally Brethren, whatsoever things are true, whatsoever things are honest, whatsoever things are just, whatsoever things are pure, whatsoever things are lovely, whatsoever things are of good Report; If there be any Vertue, and if there be any Praise, think on these things.* Chap. 1. 27. *Only let your Conversation be as it becometh the Gospel of Christ, &c. Nottingham:* Printed by *J. Collyer*, 1713. (small oct., The Dedication of 4 pp. by George Eaton, the Preface of 10 pp., + 152 pp., + a Table of 4 pp.)

See Note to Parkyns's Progymnasmata, 1714.

Away with the Fashion of this World. Come, Lord Jesus.
Being a Small LEGACY OF A Dying Minister, TO A Beloved
PEOPLE. *By the late Reverend Mr.* J. BARRET. Nottingham,
Printed by J. Collyer, and sold by R. Robinson at the Golden-Lyon
in St. Paul's Church-Yard; N. Cliff and D. Jackson, at the Bible
and three Crowns in Cheapside, London. 1713. Price Bound
Eight Pence. (16mo, of 77 pp, + 1 page of Books Sold by J.
Collier in the Long-Row, Nottingham.)

See Note to Barrett's Good Will, 1675.

The Validity of Baptism Administered by Dissenting Ministers,
&c. By a Presbyter of the Church of Christ. Nottingham:
Printed by John Collyer, &c. 1713. (pp. 22.)

By Ferdinando Shaw; see pages 10, 11, 12, and 14.
This and the cognate local tracts originated from the general Sacra-
mental controversy then debated. Lathbury in his *History of the
Nonjurors*, page 381, speaking of Roger Lawrence, the nonjuring
bishop, says, "The name of Lawrence is well known from his learned
works on the *Invalidity of Lay Baptism:* but probably it is not so
generally known, that he was a Nonjuror. His parents being
Dissenters, Lawrence was baptized in the body to which they belonged.
Entertaining doubts respecting the validity of the Act, he was led to
an extended examination of the whole subject, which issued in the
publication of his valuable and learned work: *Lay Baptism Invalid.*
The book was assailed by Dissenters, because the author had reduced
their ministers to mere laymen, which was most distasteful to the
body: it was also attacked by some members of the Church of England. He fully, as I conceive, establishes the position, that *Lay
Baptism* is not recognised by the Anglican Church, whatever may be
the decisions of the ecclesiastical courts respecting the right, which
Dissenters have to the performance of the Burial Service, in the case
of those who are baptized by their own ministers. Two Sermons
were preached at Salisbury, by Burnet, in 1710, in which Lawrence's
positions were assailed. This circumstance led him to publish, in
reply, his work on the *Sacerdotal Powers.* A few years later there
appeared another volume on *Dissenters' Baptisms.* The Bishop of
Oxford also having alluded to the subject in his Charge, Lawrence
sent forth a reply to his Lordship. These are, I believe, all the
works of this learned writer, respecting whose talents there can be no
difference of opinion, whatever may be the case concerning his views.

On the question of *Lay Baptism*, most churchmen will agree with him in sentiment. ...... Little is known of Lawrence beyond what is to be gleaned from his works, and the replies which they called forth." See also the accompanying notes for titles of books, &c.; also Nichols's Lit. An., 2nd ed., Vol. 1. page 411, note; and Index, sub voce 'Baptism.' Waterland, under 'Lay-Baptism' and 'Laurence,' Bp. Fleetwood, Abp. Bramhall, and Charles Lesley, treat of the subject.

An Answer to a Late Pamphlet Entituled The Validity of Baptism Administred by Dissenting-Ministers. Nottingham: Printed by Will. Ayscough, and Sold by John Hodges Bookseller in Derby, 1713. (pp. 28.)

Apparently Ayscough had the Orthodox, and Collyer the Dissenting, interest.

A short Attempt for preserving the MEMORY, and improving the DEATH Of Three Eminent, Aged, Ministers of CHRIST, Late of *NOTTINGHAM.* viz. Mr. William Reynolds, who died *February* the 26th, 1697-8; in his 73d year. Mr. John Whitlock, who died *December* the 4th, 1708; in his 81th year. And, Mr. John Barret, who died *October* the 30th, 1713; in his 83d year. IN TWO SERMONS, One Preach'd at the Interment of the last of these Three at *Nottingham, November* the 2d, 1713. The other formerly Preach'd, (but not publish'd) on Occasion of the Death of the second of these Three Worthies. By *JOHN WHITLOCK*, Minister of the Gospel. *Nottingham,* Printed by *J. Collyer*, and Sold by *R. Robinson* at the Golden-Lyon in St. *Paul's* Church-Yard; *N. Cliff* and *D. Jackson*, at the Bible and three Crowns in *Cheapside, London.* 1711. Price 6d.

The Dedication of this book is dated *Nottingham, New Year's Day,* 1713-14. (16mo., pp. 63 + 1 page containing the following, ' *Lately publish'd,* A small Legacy of a dying Minister, to a beloved People. By the Reverend Mr. *John Barret.* Mr. *Shaw's* Validity of Baptism administred by Dissenting Ministers. *In the Press and almost finish'd,* Select Sermons on sundry practical Subjects, by the late Reverend Mr. *Barret,* prepar'd for the Press some Years since, with a Design not to be publish'd 'till after his Death, and approv'd by several

London Ministers. A new Map of the antient Town of *Nottingham*, taken from an actual Survey of the same, with the Antiquities of the said Town and Castle, carefully extracted from the most approv'd Chronologers and Historians; in Two large Sheets of Imperial Paper. *Going to the Press,* Practical Discourses, preach'd on several New-Year's Days. By the Reverend Mr. *Shaw*. Printed and Sold by *John Collyer* in the *Long-Row, Nottingham*.')

For Reyner, Whitlock, Reynolds, Barrett, Sloss, Ryther, and many of the dissenters' names in this Catalogue, reference may be made to Carpenter's Account of Presbyterianism in Nottingham, and McAll's Historical Account of the Castle Gate meeting house, Nottingham.

A Vindication of an Answer to a Late Pamphlet entituled The Validity &c. By a Lay-Man. Nottingham: Printed by William Ayscough, for John Hodges, Bookseller in Derby. 1714.

The Invalidity of the Lay-Baptisms of Dissenting Teachers. . . . . By Henry Cantrell, M.A. Vicar of St. Alkmund's, Derby. With a Letter from the Reverend Mr. Harris. Nottingham: Printed by William Ayscough for the Bookseller of Derby, 1714. (pp. 142.)

Mr. Cantrell in 1716 published a work on the same subject:— "The Royal Martyr a true Christian; or, a Confutation of a late Assertion, *viz.* that King Charles I. had only the Lay-Baptism of a Presbyterian Teacher; with an Account of the Government of the Church of Scotland since the Reformation, shewing that Presbytery is an Innovation in that Kingdom. To which is added a particular Relation of the Solemnity of King Charles I. his Baptism, from the Heralds-office at Edinburg. By Henry Cantrell, M.A. Vicar of St. Alkmund's, Derby." Nichols's Lit. An., 2nd ed., I. 119. The subjoined note informs us that " Mr. Cantrell procured the perpetual curacy of St. Alkmund to be created into a Vicarage in 1712 ; when he was regularly presented to it by the Mayor and Aldermen of Derby. He was living there in 1760 ; in which year (at the request of Thomas Bainbrigge, Esq. high sheriff of Derbyshire) he preached (but, I believe, did not print) an Assize Sermon. I have several of his original letters to the late Dr. Pegge ; from one of which a curious anecdote relative to the civil war in 1644 is given in the History of Leicestershire, vol. III. p. 737."

Un-Episcopal Ordination and Baptism Null and Void. . . . . . .
by Higgins Harris, A.B. Curate of St. Peter's Derby. Nottingham : Printed by William Ayscough and sold by J. Hodges Bookseller in Derby. 1714. Where may be had Mr. Harris's Letter
to Mr. Cantrell. . . . . . . (pp. 44.)

The Validity of Baptism Administer'd by Dissenting Ministers :
. . . . . . By Ferdinando Shaw, M.A. Nottingham; Printed by
John Collyer, and Sold by H. Allestree, Bookseller in Derby.
1714. Price One Shilling. (pp. 120.)

Ferdinando Shaw was of Derby.

A VINDICATION OF Presbyterian Ordination ; From *SCRIP-*
TURE and *ANTIQUITY*, the Judgment of the *REFORMED*
CHURCHES, and particularly of the *CHURCH* of *ENGLAND*.
With a brief Reflection upon the Arguments offer'd by Mr.
Cantrell of Derby against it. *By a Lover of all hearty and*
charitable Protestants. To which is added, a Postscript relating
to Mr. Harris's defence of his Letter to Mr. Cantrell. *Let*
nothing be done through Strife, or Vain-glory; but in lowliness of
Mind let each esteem other better than themselves. Phil. 2. 3. In
Necessariis Unitas. In non Necessariis Libertas, In Utrisq.
Charitas. Nottingham; Printed by J. Collyer and Sold by H.
Allestree Bookseller in Derby. 1714. (Price Eight Pence.)
(oct. of 72 pp. including A Postscript.)

> At page viii., at end of Preface, mention is made 'of the Author's
> distance from the Press,' and at page 70, of 'praying that God
> would preserve and bless her Majesty *Queen Ann;' '* Note, the
> whole of the Coppy (except the Postscript) was deliver'd to the
> Printer above ten Days before the late Queens Death.' This note
> fixes the date of the Vindication at about Aug. 1, on which day
> Queen Ann died, to the great joy of the Dissenters.

ΠΡΟΓΥΜΝΑΣΜΑΤΑ. The Inn-Play : Or, Cornish-Hugg
Wrestler. Digested In a Method which teacheth to break all
Holds, and throw most Falls Mathematically. Easie to be under-

stood by all Gentlemen, &c. and of great Use to such who under-
stand the Small-Sword in Fencing. And by all Tradesmen and
Handicrafts, that have competent Knowledge of the Use of the
Stilliards, Bar, Crove-Iron or Lever, with their Hypomochlions,
Fulciments or Baits. By Sir Tho. Parkyns, of Bunny, Baronet.
Luctamur Achivis doctius unctis. Hor. Ep. Lib. 2. Ep. I. ad. Aug.
The Second Edition Corrected, with large Additions. Nottingham:
Printed and sold by Will. Ayscough in Bridlesmithgate, and
Timothy Goodwin Bookseller, over-against St. Dunstan's Church in
Fleet-street, 1714. Price One Shilling. (square octavo, pp. 64,
+ Index of pp. 8.)

The following quotation is from Timperley : but it will be seen that I
have given the titles of eight, or rather of eleven, publications issuing
from the Nottingham press during 1714, and of four printed in
Nottingham in 1713. *Newspapers,* it is confessed, were there com-
menced in 1710 by Ayscough.

'The earliest known work printed in Nottingham, bears for title
Inn-Play, or the Cornish-Hug Wrestler, 4to. By Sir Thomas Parkyns.* Printed by William Ayscough, on the west side of Bridle-
smith-gate. Mr. Ayscough was remarkable, says Deering, in his
History of Nottingham, for having first established the art of printing
in that town about the year 1710. Mr. Ayscough being unfortunate
in business, he retired, about 1715, to Bramcote, where he died, and
was buried in St. Peter's church, in Nottingham. In the south aisle,
upon a tombstone, is the following inscription : Here lye the bodies
of William Ayscough, printer and bookseller of this town, and Anne
his wife. She was the daughter of the Rev. Mr. Young, rector of
Catwick, in the county of York. He died March 2, 1719. She died
Dec. 16, 1732.

* Sir Thomas Parkyns, bart. died at Bunny, Nottinghamshire,
Feb. 29, 1741. He was founder of the present noble house of Ran-
cliffe.' (Title now extinct.)

The Rev. C. B. Norcliffe of Langton Hall informs me that Mr,
William Askough and Mrs. Ann Younge were married at Catwick, 11
April, 1709. He believes that her mother Elizabeth, was a Wilford
of Co. Kent, grand-daughter of Sir Thomas Wilford by Elizabeth
daughter of Isaac Bargrave, Dean of Canterbury. He writes, 'Who
Ayscough was I cannot say ;' Thoroton shews that there was previously a family of that name connected with Nuthall near Nottm.

The Private Christian's Reasons For Stated Communion with a
DISSENTING Congregation. I. Pet. 3. Part of the 15th and

16th Verses . . . . and be ready always to give an Answer to every Man that asketh you the Reason of the Hope that is in you, with Meekness and Fear. Having a good Conscience; that whereas they speak Evil of you, as of Evil Doers, they may be ashamed that falsly accuse your good Conversation in Christ. *Nottingham:* Printed by *John Collyer,* in the *Long-Row.* 1714. (16mo. of pp. 16.)

AN ESSAY UPON Vocal MUSICK, WHEREIN is amply and clearly demonstrated by RULE and EXAMPLE, whatever is necessary for the Attainment to the true and perfect Knowledge of that Science. Set forth by way of DIALOGUE, AND intended for the Use and Benefit of altrue Lovers of divine MUSICK. By *DANIEL ROBINSON,* Philomusic. Te, Magne rerum conditor, & tuas sonabo Laudes, factaque posteris Miranda prodam, dum recurret per calidos mihi Sanguis artus. Buch. NOTTINGHAM: Printed by *J.* COLLYER for the Author, and sold by *B.* FARNWORTH in *Newark, H.* ALLESTREE in *Derby,* and *C.* ROTTEN in *Harborough,* BOOKSELLERS. 1715. (Price two Shillings.) (oct., pp. 8 of Title, Dedication, Preface, and Contents; + pp. 154.)

A COLLECTION OF CHOICE *PSALM-TUNES* IN Three and Four PARTS: WITH New and Easie PSALM-TUNES, HYMNS, ANTHEMS, and Spiritual SONGS, composed by the best MASTERS; with the *Contra* and *Treble* in the same *Cliff* that the *Tenor* is in. By JOHN *and* JAMES GREEN. *The Third Edition, with large Additions.* PSALM cxlvi., Ver. 1. *Praise the Lord, O my Soul, while I live will I Praise the Lord: Yea, as long as I have any Being, I will sing Praises unto my God. Nottingham:* Printed by *William Ayscough* for *Joseph Turner,* Bookseller in *Sheffield, Yorkshire;* and sold by *J. Sprint,* at the Bell in *Little-Britain, London.* 1715. [Oct.; title 1 p., Preface by James Green 1 p., The Introduction 14 pp., + 152 pp.]

Remarks on two Sermons, of Mr. Ferdinando Shaw, &c. Nottingham: Printed by W. Ayscough in Bridlesmithgate. 1715. (pp. 16.)

* A SERMON AGAINST MURMURING, Preach'd at The Assizes, at St. *Mary's Nottingham, Aug.* 16. 1715. Before the Right Honourable the Lord Chief Baron Dodd, and Mr. Justice Pratt. By *SAMUEL BERDMORE*, M.A. Vicar of St. *Mary's Nottingham*, and Prebendary of *Southwell. Publish'd at the request of the High Sheriff, and the Gentlemen of the Grand Jury. LONDON*, Printed for William Ward Bookseller in *Nottingham*, and J. Varnam and J. Osborn at the *Oxford-Arms* in *Lombard-Street.* MDCC.XV. Price Three Pence. (oct., 24 pp.)

The Wonders of the Year 1716 .... By a Native of *L. M. W. Y.* ..... Nottingham : Printed for W. Ward, 1716. (Octavo, 24 pp.)

* A SERMON Preach'd before the Artillery Company of *Nottingham*, ON Monday the 28th of *May*, 1716. BEING HIS Majesty's Birth-Day ; AT St. Mary's in *Nottingham*. By Samuel Berdmore, M.A. Vicar of St. *Mary's*, and Prebendary of the Collegiate Church of *Southwell* in *Nottinghamshire. LONDON*, Printed for John Collyer Bookseller in *Nottingham*. M.DCC.XVI. (Price Four Pence). (oct. 8 pp. of Title, Dedication, and advertisement; + 24 pp.)

The advertisement is entitled *BOOKS lately printed, and sold by* William Ward, *Bookseller in* Nottingham, and contains notices of Berdmore's Sermons of July 23, 1710, and Aug 14, 1715; of The Wonders of the Year 1716; and of Practical Discourses on all the Parts and Offices of the Liturgy of the Church of *England.* Wherein are laid open the Harmony, Excellency and Usefulness of its Composure. In four Volumes. Useful for all Families. By *Matthew Hole*, D.D. Rector of *Exeter-College* in *Oxford.*
Ward seems to have been a bookseller who employed printers in London and Nottingham ; in the latter place Collyer probably did his work.

The real Christian's Character and comfortable End consider'd and improv'd. In a Funeral Sermon .... Mrs. Rebekah Woolley .... Derby .... By Jos. Rogerson. Nottingham : Printed by J. Collyer. in the Long-Row, 1716. (pp. 28.)

A Practical and Grammatical Introduction to the Latin Tongue. By Sr. Thomas Parkyns of Bunny, Bart. For the Use of His Grand-Son and of Bunny-School. The Second Edition, with many Additions. Nottingham : Printed by William Ayscough in Bridlesmithgate. 1716. (oct. pp. 39, + 39.)

The Garland of Merriment : Containing Three New Songs . . . . Nottingham : Printed by William Ayscough in Bridlesmithgate. (pp. 8.)

Internal evidence fixes the date 1716-7.

Counterfeit Loyalty Displayed : . . . . A Sermon Preached at All-Saints-Church in Derby, Upon the 30th of January, (1716-17). By the Reverend Dr. Hutchinson . . . . Nottingham, Printed for H. Allestree Bookseller in Derby. (1717.) (pp. 24).

EIGHTEEN SERMONS ON *Practical Subjects.* By the Reverend John Killingbeck B.D. Late Vicar of *Leeds*, and Prebendary of *York*, and sometimes Fellow of *Jesus-College* in *Cambridge*. NOTTINGHAM : Printed by Will. Ayscough, for John Swale, Bookseller, and Sold by him at his Shops in *Leeds*, and *Wakefield;* and by John Sprint, Bookseller, at the *Bell* in *Little-Britain, London.* MDCCXVII. (14 pp. of Title, Dedication, Abp. of York's letter, and Contents; + 382 pp., + 1 page of Errata.)

A PRACTICAL and GRAMMATICAL INTRODUCTION TO THE *Latine* Tongue. BY Sir. *THOMAS PARKYNS OF BUNNY*, Bart. For the Use of his GRAND-SON, and of *Bunny* SCHOOL. The Third EDITION, with many Additions. *NOTTINGHAM :* Printed by *WILLIAM WARD*, and Sold by *Timothy Goodwin*, over-against St. *Dunstan's Church* in *Fleet-Street, London ; John Ward* in *Leicester ; Henry Allestree* in *Derby ;* and *Francis Hildyard* in *York*, Booksellers. MDCCXVII. [oct., 109 pp., + 1 p. of errata.]

Aristarchus Anti-Bentleianus QUADRAGINTA SEX BENTLEII ERRORES SUPER Q. HORATII FLACCI Odarum LIBRO Primo Spissos

Nonnullos, Et Erubescendos : ITEM per Notas universas in *Latinitate* Lapsus fœdissimos *Nonaginta* ostendens. Autore RICHARDO JOHNSON, Ludi-Magistro NOTTINGHAMIENSI. *Quid Romæ faciam mentiri nescio; librum Si malus est nequeo laudare et poscere ?* Juv. *Nec reniam insulsis sed honorem et præmia posci.* Hor. NOTTINGHAMIÆ, Typis *Gulielmi Ayscough,* Impensis Autoris apud *Samuelem Keble* ad Insigne *Capitis Turcici* vico vulgo dicto *Fleet-Street,* veno positus 1717. (Preface of 18 pp., + 112 pp., + Pars Secunda, title + 116 pp.)

Monk's Life of Bentley, Vol. I., page 8. "Among the students of the same year with Bentley, I find some names of no small celebrity : Samuel Garth . . . . ; John Dennis . . . . ; Richard Johnson, of the same college as Bentley, was also his contemporary ; and I conjecture him to be the person afterwards master of Nottingham School, and author of *Grammatical Commentaries, Noctes Nottinghamicæ,* and *Aristarchus Anti-Bentleianus.* This indentity, which there seems little reason to doubt, may help to account for the personal rancour displayed against Bentley in the latter production ; which is inexplicable but upon the supposition of some previous intercourse. Johnson's spleen might have been the offspring of a feud begun at the University, or of mortification at the neglect of old acquaintance by his more fortunate fellow-collegian." The note appended reads as follows :— "Johnson in his 'Grammatical Commentaries,' styles himself M.A., and Mr. Gilbert Wakefield, who gives some account of him in the Memoirs of his own life, says, that 'he could not find out which University had the honour of his education.' Bentley's contemporary, Richard Johnson, is the only graduate of the name, either at Oxford or Cambridge, who could be the Nottingham schoolmaster. He proceeded indeed no further than his degree of B.A. But there have been many instances of persons who, having only taken that first degree, afterwards intimated their academical education by assuming the title of M.A. to which they had no claim ; probably from a dislike of the juvenile notion connected with the term 'Bachelor of Arts.'"

See also Monk, ii. 3, ii. 6., for Johnson's 'burlesque criticism' from the *Aristarchus* p. 109. ii. 7 ; "Johnson did not very long survive his exhibition in the character of *Aristarchus :* he was overtaken by some mental malady which proved the precursor of his melancholy fate. Little more is known respecting him, but that in the year 1720 he drowned himself in the meadows adjacent to Nottingham." (G. W., 1. 28, ed. 1504.) In 1721, as shewn below.

Monk, i. 5. Bentley's tutor was the Rev. Joseph Johnston ; in the note,—"Bentley's tutor, when he took his degree of B.A. in 1664,

3

spelled his name *Johnson*. The reader of these memoirs will perhaps be struck with the coincidence which associates so many persons of the name of *Johnson* with Bentley's history."

"In 1682 Bentley bade adieu to Spalding (where he was succeeded by Mr. Walter Johnson)."

In ii. 59, mention is made of 'Dr. James Johnson of Trinity Hall, a warm partizan of Bentley.'

Probably the link between Bentley and Richard Johnson may be found at Spalding, with which a numerous and learned family of the latter name was connected. See Nichols's Lit. An., under 'Johnson.'

Johnson and the Trustees once went to law, I believe on the question of his ejection for incompetency, and on the trial the opposing counsel said of the schoolmaster that much learning had made him mad; the natural retort was ready, that however mad Mr. Abney might shew himself, no one could be got to think that the infliction in his case had proceeded from study. Johnson proved his competency and won his case by producing in court a certificate of ability to teach, which he had obtained from the trustees under pretence of applying for another appointment. Mr. Nelson of Great Limber, in conversation with me, lately attached the latter part of the story to Parson Leeke, vicar of Fulstow near Louth, 40 years ago a noted clerical dealer in piebald horses and ponies, who similarly outwitted his parishioners at the Bishop's visitation at Caistor.

Poor Johnson was found drowned, and the register of his burial at St. Nicholas's, Nottm., reads, '1721. Mr Richard Johnson Clerk (Author of ye Gramat. Coment) bur^d Oct. 26.'

Noctes Nottinghamicæ OR Cursory Objections Against the SYN-TAX OF THE COMMON-GRAMMAR, In Order to obtain a Better: Design'd in the mean time for the Use of Schools. By RICHARD JOHNSON, M.A. Author of the *Grammatical Commentaries*, and *Aristarchus Anti-Bentlianus.* Master of the Free-School in *Nottingham. Quis inepti Tam patiens libri, tam ferreus ut teneat se?* Juv. *Nottingham :* Printed for HENRY CLEMENTS at the *Half-Moon* in St. *Paul's* Church-Yard, *London.* 1718. (Title of 1 page; + Dedication to William, Abp. of York, 6 pp; + the Preface to the School-Masters, 21 pp.; + 94 pp.; + Errata 1 page.)

Probably printed by Ayscough.

JOHN WILDS Two Penny ACCIDENCE; Corn without Chaff. Manifestly Shewing how to form Verbs without Mood and

Tense; and Adjectives and Nouns by Terminations only; with single Words and Letters for Signs of Case and Gender. As it was usual in his School: Put forth for the Benefit of his Scholars, such as are now School-Masters. *Particularly For* Thomas Smith *School-Master in* Gotham. *The Fool Answer'd and, not answer'd according to his Folly.* Commend it or come mend it, The Preservation of Folly, in its Integrity being the Policy of Ignorance; *Lilly's* Defamation, turn'd to his Renown, which none can perceive who go not out of their wits; *to wit,* Beyond 24 Letters, which is the utmost Capacity of *English* Understanding. Nottingham: *Printed by* Will. Ayscough *in* Woolpacklane, *for the Author* John Wild *of* Little-Leak. (12mo. of 36 pp.)

Barker of Thetford has marked my copy as 'circa 1720;' I have placed it in the previous year, as William Ayscough died March 2, 1719, N.S.

Johnson was Master of the Nottm. Grammar School from 1707 to 1718, and the above is probably a parody on his *Noctes Nottinghamicæ,* by Bentley, Leedes, Parkyns, or Samuel Jebb, in revenge for the attack on Bentley in the *Aristarchus;* compare John Wild's title-page with Bp. Monk's belief that Johnson had been Bentley's youthful contemporary at St. John's College, Cambridge.

REMARKS UPON Mr. *Peniston Booth's* Friendly Advice to the ANABAPTISTS; In ANSWER to Mr. Hall's Antidote, Wherein is shewn 1*st.* How unfairly Mr. *Booth* has done by Mr. *Hall.* And, 2*dly.* By them he affects to call Anabaptists in a more General Respect. And, 3*dly.* That the Arguments he has advanced for Infant Baptism are insufficient. And, *Lastly.* Some Friendly Advice offer'd to Mr. *Booth* by way of Conclusion. By JOHN HURSTHOUSE of *Croft,* in the County of *Lincoln.* Search the Scriptures for in them ye think ye have eternal Life, and they are they which testify of me, John 5. 39. Which Things also we speak, not in the Words which man's Wisdom teacheth, but which the Holy Ghost teacheth; comparing spiritual Things with spiritual, I. Cor. 2. 17. For it is written I will destroy the Wisdom of the wise, and will bring to nothing the understanding of the prudent, I. Cor. 1. 19. Where is the wise? Where is the Scribe? Where is the Disputer of this World? Hath not God made foolish the Wisdom of this World? I. Cor. 1. 20. Nottingham: Printed by

J. Collyer near the . . . . . . ('The rest cut off. Octavo. The Title,
A Letter to the Author from G. Eaton, dated September 22. 1719,
and the Epistle to the Reader occupy 12 pages; + pp. 151.)

THE PSALM-SINGERS DELIGHTFUL Companion Containing great variety of new PSALM-TUNES with a Choice Collection of HYMNS In Two Three and Four Parts And over them
is set what distance each begins with the Bass. To make it more
plain have reduced the C Cliff to G solrent Cliff natural : To attain
this delightfull Art, have set a Gamut divided into all the seven
Parts of Musick, with Lessons for Tuning the Voice, to find Mi in
all the usual Places of Flats and Sharps, and for transposing Mi
through all the seven Keys, with proper Directions for learning the
same, being an easier Method to the Art of Psalmody then hath
been before published. By John Clay, of NOTTINGHAM.
Psalm 47. Ver, 6. 7. *Sing Praises to God sing praises: Sing
Praises unto our King sing Praises. For God is King of all the
Earth, sing ye Praises with Understanding* NOTTINGHAM : Printed
and sold by *Anne Ayscough*, and *J. Clay*. MDCCXX. (small
oct., pp. 48.)

> "In country parishes, where the people have not the aid of an
> instrument to guide them, such young men and women as nature has
> endowed with an ear and a tolerable voice, are induced to learn to
> sing by book, as they call it; and in this they are generally assisted
> by some poor ignorant man, whom the poring over Ravenscroft and
> Playford has made to believe, that he is as able a proficient in
> psalmody as either of those authors. Such men as these assume the
> title of singing masters and lovers of divine music, and are the
> authors of those collections which are extant in the world, and are
> distinguished by the titles of—"David's Harp new strung and tuned,"
> "The Harmony of Zion," "The Psalm-singer's Companion,"—and
> others of the like kind, to an incredible number." Sir John Hawkins's
> History of Music, (Novello,) Vol II, page 695.

*A very short and plain Account of the Principles and Duties of
the Christian Religion.* A SERMON On *Acts* 16. 31. *By* Ann.
Jeacock *NOTTINGHAM*, Printed by John Collyer at the *Hen-
Cross*. 1721 (oct. of 33 pp.)

A COPY OF A POLL Taken for the County of *Nottingham*,
The 4th. and 5th. Days of APRIL, Anno Dom, 1722, BEFORE
John Grundy, Esq ; HIGH-SHERRIFF for the said County. NOT-
TINGHAM: Printed by ANNE AYSCOUGH in Bridlesmithgate.
(oct. of 84 pp.)

> Lord Howe and Sir Robert Sutton elected.
> Anne Ayscough died Dec. 16, 1732 ; see page 13.

* A DISCOURSE OF THE COVENANT of GRACE : Wherein the
Definition, Nature, Excellency, Seals, Mediator, and Perpetuity
thereof, with several other Things concerning the same, are briefly considered. By *T. Davye.* — *He is the Mediator of a better Covenant,
which was established upon better Promises,* Heb. 8. 6. *LONDON,*
Printed by J. DARBY in *Bartholomew-Close,* and sold by JOHN
WARD in *Leicester,* WILLIAM WARD in *Nottingham,* THOMAS HURT
in *Coventry,* and — FOWLER in *Northampton.* M.DCC.XXIII.
(oct.; Title, Preface, and verses occupy 8 pp.; + 85 pp.; + The
contents, 2 pp.)

* *The Justice and Religion of Magistrates,* Considered in a
SERMON Preached in the Parish-Church of St. *Mary, Nottingham,* BEFORE THE MAYOR and ALDERMEN, On *Michaelmas* Day
1724. By *JOHN DISNEY,* Vicar of the said Church. *And published at the Request of some that heard it. LONDON:* Printed
for JOHN OSBORN, at the *Oxford-Arms* in *Lombard-Street;* and
WILLIAM WARD, Bookseller in *Nottingham,* 1724. (oct. of 27 pp.)

* QUERIES AND REASONS OFFER'D by Sir *THOMAS PARKYNS,*
Of BUNNY, Bar.t why the COUNTY-HALL, GOAL, &c. should be built
in the County of *Nottingham,* and on the new purchas'd ground for
that very Purpose, and not in the Market-Place of the Town, and
County of the Town of *Nottingham,* and out of the County at large :
And why he could not join with his brethren the Justices of the
Peace, in Signing the Order of Sessions at *Rufford, April* the 24th,
1724. WITH The Addition of SUBORDINATION ; or, an Essay on
Servants, their Rates of Wages, and the Great Convenience which will
accrue to every County, by Recording with all the Chief Constables,
&c. of the same. *Difficile est Satyram non scribere.* Juv. Lib. 1.

The THIRD EDITION, with Emendations and large Additions. *LONDON*, Printed by HENRY WOODFALL, at *Elzevir's Head* without *Temple-Bar*, and Sold by THOMAS WEEKES, Bookseller, in *Westminster-Hall*; JOHN COLLYER, Printer, at the *Hen-Cross* in *Nottingham*; and HUMPHREY WAINWRIGHT of *Bunny* in the said County. M.DCC.XXIV. (square oct. of 40 pp., with 'ODE Ad honorabilem Thomam Parkyns, Baronettum. *Nottinghamiæ* Apud *Johannem Collyer*, 1724,' prefixed to page 7, making 4 additional folio folding pages.)

> Sir Thomas, a great patron of wrestling, died in 1741; his statue, representing a wrestler, stands on the north side of Bunney chancel, on the inside.

THE WONDERS OF THE PEAK. By CHARLES COTTON, Esq; *Barbara Pyramidum sileat miracula Memphis.* Mart. Epig. NOTTINGHAM: Printed by JOHN COLLYER, and sold by H. Cantrel and H. Allestree in Derby, J. Bradley and S. Gunter in Chesterfield, and Mr. Whitworth in Manchester, Booksellers. 1725. (small square oct., title of 1 page, + 71 pp.)

> The title of this edition is partly rubricated.

* A VINDICATION OF THE ANSWER TO THE SIXTH QUESTION IN THE *Assembly's shorter Catechism,* In ANSWER to a late Pamphlet, INTITLED, *An Address to* PROTESTANT DISSENTERS; *or, An Enquiry into the Grounds of their Attachment to the* Assembly's *Catechism.* By *JAMES SLOSS,* M.A. *LONDON,* Printed by H. WOODFALL, for the AUTHOR; and sold by J. OSWALD at the *Rose* and *Crown,* and J. DAVIDSON, at the *Golden Lion,* both in the *Poultry;* and JOHN MURRAY Book-binder in *Nottingham.* 1728. (Price Six-pence.) [octavo, title of 1 page, + 37 pp.]

> In all likelihood this tract is mis-dated, and should be placed under 1735, being as it is, an answer to Bourn's ADDRESS to *PROTESTANT DISSENTERS*, which appeared in 1736.

THE Excellent USE OF PSALMODY. WITH A Course of SINGING PSALMS for Half a Year. BEGINNING On the First

Sunday in *January*, and again on the First Sunday in *July :* And also Proper PSALMS for particular DAYS and OCCASIONS. BOTH Taken out of the DIRECTIONS given by *EDMUND* Lord Bishop of *LONDON* to the CLERGY of his Diocese, in the Year 1724. With an Addition since made by his Lordship, of PSALMS proper to be sung by *CHARITY-CHILDREN* in the Church, on the Days of COLLECTION Publish'd at length by the Approbation of the Clergy. To which is added, A Collection of choice Hymns, with a short Introduction, by Way of Dialogue, for the Use and Benefit of all true Lovers of Psalmody. By *R. W.* a Lover of Divine Musick. *Nottingham:* Printed and Sold by *George Ayscough,* and *Richard Willis* in *Bearwood-Lane.* MDCCXXXIV. (octavo; title, two prefaces, and (*a*) title to the Introduction occupy 8 pp.; + 56 pp; + The Introduction, unpaged, 16 pp. (*a*) A 𝔭𝔞𝔱𝔥 𝔴𝔞𝔶 TO Vocal Musick : OR, AN, INTRODUCTION TO Lovers and Learners of *Psalmody* Wherein is amply and clearly demonstrated by RULE and EXAMPLE, whatever is Necessary for the Attainment to the true and perfect Knowledge of that Science Set forth by way of Dialogue, for the Benefit of Young Practitioners. By a Lover of DIVINE MUSICK. The Second Edition, with Additions. *NOTTINGHAM:* Printed by GEORGE AYSCOUGH.)

> The Deering MS. states that Anne Ayscough was made guardian of her son George, 17 yrs old, in 1732.

SERIOUS ADVICE OF A *PARENT* TO HIS CHILDREN, CONCERNING THE *ERRORS* of the DAY. By a TRADESMAN. Math. VII. 15. *Beware of false Prophets,* &c. Math. XVI. 6. *Then* JESUS *said unto them, take heed and beware of the Leaven of the Pharisees, and of the Sadduces.* 2 Cor. XI. 3. *But I fear lest by any Means, as the Serpent beguiled Eve through his Subtilty, so your Minds should be corrupted from the Simplicity that is in* CHRIST. Col. ii. 4. *And this I say, least any Man should beguile you with inticing Words.* *NOTTINGHAM:* Printed by *Tho. Collyer,* near the *Hen-Cross.* M.DCC.XXX.IV. (16mo., octavo size, 94 pp.)

* *The great Duty of doing as you would be done by, explain'd and recommended,* IN A SERMON PREACH'D at the Assizes held at

Nottingham Before the Honourable Mr. Baron *COMYNS*, and Mr. Justice *REEVE*, On *July* 25. 1735. By *JOHN FOSS*, A.M. Rector of *Castleford*, in the County of *YORK*. *Hic Murus aheneus esto.* Hor. *Publish'd at the Request of the* High-Sheriff and Grand-Jury. *LONDON:* Printed for *William Ward*, Bookseller in *Nottingham;* and sold by *Tho. Longman*, at the *Ship* in *Pater-noster-Row.* M DCC XXXV. (oct., 28 pp.)

* THE TRUE NARRATIVE OF THE CASE OF *JOSEPH RAWSON*, Who was Excommunicated by the Congregation of Protestant Dissenters, meeting at *Castle-Gate, Nottingham;* Signed by the Pastors and other Office-Bearers of that CHURCH. Together with *A Prefatory Discourse,* and *a Plea for the Right of Religious Societies to excommunicate* Heretical *and* Unruly *Members.* By James Sloss, *M.A. LONDON:* Printed by *H. Woodfall,* for the Author; and sold by *J. Oswald,* at the *Rose* and *Crown,* and *J. Davidson,* at the *Golden Lyon,* both in the *Poultry; Alex. Cruden,* under the *Royal Exchange;* and *Thomas Collyer,* Bookseller in *Nottingham.* (Price One Shilling.) [Oct., title of 1 page; + 70 pp.] No date, 1737 or 1738.

This 'True Narrative' was preceded in 1737, by 'A Narrative of Mr. Joseph Rawson's Case, &c. . . . with a Prefatory Discourse in Defence of the Common Rights of Christians,' (the Pref. Disc. was by John Taylor, of Norwich), printed in London; also preceded, as appears by the Advertisement at the end of the 'True Narrative,' by 'An Address to Protestant Dissenters: &c. By a Protestant Dissenter (viz. Bourn). . . . . London . . . . 1736.' This last was answered by Sloss's Vindication, which came after the 'True Narrative.'

Joseph Rawson was excommunicated July 9, 1736. The following extract is from McAll's Historical Notices:—'In 1733, *Mr. James Sloss, M.A.*, was appointed Mr. Bateson's co-pastor. Mr. Sloss was a minister of the church of Scotland, and (as such) a Presbyterian; but it was stipulated on his becoming pastor, that he should not attempt any alteration in the mode of church-government. He was very highly respected for his learning and ability. Several published works attested his diligence; and among them, one of great value on the doctrine of the Trinity. Mr. S. held the pastoral office at Castle Gate for nearly forty years. Very shortly after his resignation, he died suddenly, on or about the first of May, 1772. The newspapers of that day record his name in terms of high respect, and intimate that his death was a loss to the poor and needy of every persuasion;' page 84. ' The principal occurrence which marked the joint ministry of Mr. Bateson and Mr. Sloss, was the exclusion of one of the most prominent members of the church for Arianism—a circumstance which occasioned numerous pamphlets, and a protracted controversy, spreading beyond the neighbourhood to parties at a distance. The first notice of this affair in the Church Book reads as follows :— " May 25, 1736. Some time was spent in prayer and humiliation, to ask direction of God how to proceed about Mr. Joseph Rawson, a member with us, who was suspected of having imbibed the Arian notion, and denying the supreme Deity of Jesus Christ;" ' page 85. ' It has also been noticed, that the first enlargement of Castle Gate Meeting, was occasioned by an influx of persons from the previously orthodox Presbyterian Congregation. This occurred in 1738;' page 99.

Apropos of the general controversy, reference may be made to The Scholar Armed, Wardlaw's Socinian Controversy, Waterland by Van Mildert, and Dr. Pye Smith.

AN ESSAY ON *CHRIST'S Fear of Death :* OR, AN Appeal to the Equity AND Common Sense of Mankind, From the Judgment of the Independent CHURCH AT *NOTTING-HAM.* JOHN, XVI. 2. *They shall put you out of their synagogues.* MATT. X. 23. *When they persecute ye in one city, flee ye to another. LONDON :* Printed for J. Roberts in *Warwick-Lane ;* E. Nutt, at the *Royal-Exchange ;* and A. Dod, at the *Peacock* without *Temple-Bar ;* and Sold by Anne Ayscough in *Nottingham ;* and J. Roe in *Derby.* 1737. [Price Six-Pence] (octavo, 40 pp.)

The preface, of 10 pp., is by a friend of the Author, and takes the side of Rawson.

This Essay is in fact a Sermon, preached at Castle-Gate at the solicitation of Mr. Floyd who was Assistant to Mr. Bateson 1730-3.

* A Further defence of the common rights of *CHRIST-IANS,* And of the Sufficiency and Perfection of *SCRIPTURE,* without the Aid of *Human Schemes, Creeds, Confessions,* &c. Occasioned by Mr. Sloss's pretended *True Narrative of the Case* of Joseph Rawson, *who was excommunicated by the Congregation*

4

of PROTESTANT DISSENTERS, meeting in Castle-gate, Nottingham.
By *JOHN TAYLOR*, Minister of the Gospel at *Norwich*, and late
of *Kirkstead*, in *Lincolnshire;* Author of *The Prefatory Discourse
to* Rawson's *Narrative.* Prov. XXX. 5, 6. *Every Word of God
is pure: He is a Shield unto them that put their Trust in him.
Add thou not to his Words lest he reprove thee.* LONDON:
Printed for RICHARD HETT, at the *Bible* and *Crown* in the *Poultry;*
and sold by W. WARD and J. COLLYER, in *Nottingham*, and J. ROE,
in *Derby.* 1738. (oct., 79 pp., + 1 of advertisements.)

*The Things that make for Peace and Edification amongst
Christians* RECOMMENDED IN A SERMON Preached at an
ASSEMBLY OF MINISTERS At the High-Pavement in
NOTTINGHAM June 28, 1738. And published at their unani-
mous Request By J. CLEGG, *V.D.M.* M.D. *NOTTINGHAM:*
Printed by *Tho. Collyer*, and sold by J. ROE in *Derby*, S.
SIMMONS in *Sheffield*, and J. SLATER in *Chesterfield.* (Price 6d.)
M DCC XXXVIII. [Oct., 42 pp.; on Rom. XIV. 19.]

I quote two passages, one from p. 29, as shewing his views; ' Had
one of our Champions for *Orthodoxy* been in his Place, he would
have assum'd another Air, and have dictated in a loftier Tone. But
St. Paul knew better; he knew the World and human Nature too
well to do that; he knew the People he dealt with, could not bear
the assuming Air of Superiority; he knew that reasonable Creatures
should be reasonably treated, and that gentle Methods would better
open their Minds to Conviction, and sooner find the way to their
Hearts. And this all Ministers and private Christians, that have to
do with such as they think mistaken, will find too, if they can but
bear with them, treat them kindly, and use gentle Means and rational
Methods for their Conviction.' At page 34 he says, ' I remember
with Pleasure, how my Heart has been affected by reading some
Papers deliver'd at Conferences in this Town, by that serious and
excellent Christian *Mr. Joseph Barret*, and others.'
Watt mentions also a Sermon on Matt. XVI. 18, 1731, 8vo.;
Funeral Sermon, 1736.

A COPY OF THE LETTERS *Lately Publish'd*, Occasion'd by
Mr. Sloss's Circular Letter. The SECOND EDITION. To which is
added A *LETTER* To the Reverend Mr. *John Alwood*, Mr.

Richard Bateson, Mr. *Ogle Radford.* Which last LETTER may be had single. NOTTINGHAM: Printed by *Tho. Collyer*, and sold by *J. Roe* in Derby, *T. Warren* in Birmingham, and *S. Simmons* in Sheffield. 1738. (oct., title, + 11 pp, + A Letter of 12 pp.)

Catalogus Stirpium, &c. OR, A Catalogue of PLANTS Naturally growing and commonly cultivated in divers Parts of *England*, More especially about *Nottingham.* CONTAINING, The most known *Latin* and *English* Names of the several PLANTS, the Tribe they belong to, the Time of their flowering, and of those which are either Officinals, or otherwise of any known Efficacy, such Virtues are briefly mentioned as may be depended upon. With an *English* Index. To which is added, for the Benefit of the *English* Reader, a general Distribution of PLANTS, according to Mr. RAY, an Explanation of some *Botanical* and *Physical* Terms, and an Alphabetical List of PLANTS in Flower for every Month in the Year, together with short Directions when to gather any Parts of them. *Medicus omnium Stirpium (si fieri potest) Peritiam habeat consulo: Sin minus plurium Saltem quibus frequenter utimur.* GALEN. *Lib.* 1. Antidot. By C. DEERING, M.D. NOTTINGHAM: Printed for the AUTHOR, by G. AYSCOUGH, and sold by C. RIVINGTON, at the Bible and Crown in St. *Paul's* Church-yard, *London.* 1738. (octavo. Title and Dedication each of 1 page; TO THE READER 14 pp.; + *Abreviated* NAMES *explain'd,* 2 pp; + Catalogus Stirpium, &c. 231 pp.; + English INDEX 9 pp; + An Alphabetical LIST 7 pp; + *ERRATA* 2 pp; + *General Distribution,* 24 pp.

Charles Deering was a Native of Saxony, and died in poverty in the year 1749.

Derby Silk-Mill. Attempted in Miltonick Verse. . . . . . . By the Reverend Mr. John Brailsford A.M. Rector of Kirby in Nottinghamshire. Nottingham: Printed for the Author by George Ayscough 1739. (folio, 6 pp.)

I have Thirteen sermons on various subjects by the late J. Brailsford, A.M. Head Master of the Free-School, in Birmingham, Vicar of North-Wheatley, in Nottinghamshire, And Chaplain to the Right Honourable Lord Middleton. Birmingham, 1776.

THE WONDERS OF THE PEAK : By *CHARLES COTTON,*
Esq; *Barbara Pyramidum sileat miracula Memphis.* Mart. Epig.
The Second Edition. *NOTTINGHAM :* Printed by *Tho. Collyer,*
and sold by the Booksellers of York, Sheffield, Chesterfield, Mansfield, Derby, and Newark. M.DCC.XLIV. (small oct. of 60 pp.)

Collyer's business descended thus;—Coilyer, Creswell, Burbage,
Stretton, Hicklin, Oliver, Forman. Fo.' the first link in the state-
ment I am indebted to the relict of the late Jonathan Dunn, who had
it from Mrs. Pepper, who was Collyer's daughter. Creswell derived
the paper, afterwards called the Nottingham Journal, from George
Ayscough.

A New LATIN GRAMMAR, adapted to the Capacities of
Young Scholars ; Comprising every Thing In the Art, Necessary
for Grammar Schools. With short, easy, and proper Examples To
all, and every part of, the Rules In SYNTAX. By the Rev. Mr.
Henson, Master of the Free-School in *Nottingham.* Hæc de
Grammaticâ, quam brevissimè potui; non ut omnia dicerem, sec-
tatus (quod infinitum erat;) sed ut maximè necessaria. *Quinctil.
de Institut. Orat.* Lib. 10. *NOTTINGHAM:* Printed for the
Author, and sold by J. Rivington, in St. *Paul's* Church-yard,
London; and G. Ayscough, in *Bridlesmithgate,* Nottingham.
M,DCC,XLIV. (16mo. Title, Dedication and Preface of 11 pp.,
+ 224 pp.)

Mr. John Henson was appointed Usher in 1724, Master in 1731.

* A Sermon Preached, On Occasion of the Fast, *April* 11,
1744; At *Castlegate, Nottingham:* From Matt. viii. 25. *And his
Disciples came to him, and awoke him, saying, Lord, save us; we
perish.* By *JAMES SLOSS,* M.A. Published at the Desire of
the Congregation. *LONDON:* Printed by *H. WOODFALL,*
without *Temple-Bar :* For John Oswald, at the *Rose* and *Crown;*
and Joseph Davidson, at the *Angel,* both in the *Poultry;* and
Joseph Heath, Bookseller, in *Nottingham.* 1744. (Price Six-
pence.) [oct. pp. 39.]

The Evangelical History and Harmony. by Matthew Pilkington, LL.B. . . . . . . London. Sold by . . . . . G. Ayscough at Nottingham. . . . . . . MDCCXLVII.

THE *GOUTY MAN'S* Companion, OR A *Dietetical* and *Medicinal* Regimen: AS WELL On the *Approach*, as in the *State*, AND In the *Declination* of the *GOUT*, WITH Preventative Directions, in the Intervals of the *Paroxysms*. By *JOHN CHESHIRE*, MB. of *Leicester*. *Experto Crede*. *NOTTINGHAM:* Printed by G. Ayscough, for the Author, and Sold by the Booksellers in Town and Country. MDCCXLVII. (Large 16mo.; Title, *DEDICATION, The* PREFACE, and ERRATA, occupy 18 pp.; + 97 pp.; + AN INDEX To the Preface, 4 pp.; + AN INDEX To the BOOK, 13 pp.)

A Rational Concordance, Or an Index to the Bible . . . . . . by Matthew Pilkington, LL.B. Nottingham: Printed by, and for, George Ayscough, MDCCXLIX. (small quarto, 192 pp.)

NOTTINHAMIA VETUS ET NOVA OR AN HISTORICAL ACCOUNT OF THE ANCIENT AND PRESENT STATE OF THE TOWN OF NOTTINGHAM. GATHER'D From the Remains of Antiquity and Collected from Authentic Manuscripts and Ancient as well as Modern Historians. ADORN'D with beautiful Copper-Plates with An APPENDIX, Containing Besides Extracts of Wills and Deeds relating to CHARITIES, Diverse other Curious PAPERS. By *CHARLES DEERING*, M.D. *NOTTINGHAM:* Printed by and for, George Ayscough, & Thomas Willington. MDCCLI. (octavo, quarto size; Title and *DEDICATION*, 6 pp.; + *To the* READER, 1 p.; + The INTRODUCTION, 13 pp.; CONTENTS, 1 page; + 370 pp.)

> The Rev. Samuel Ayscough, F.S.A., the Shakspearian, born 1745, died Oct. 30, 1804, was the son of the above George Ayscough.

* *DAVID'S* Harp well Tuned: OR A BOOK OF PSALMODY. CONTAINING Variety of PSALM-TUNES, BOTH FOR THE Common and Particular Measures; WITH CHANTING-TUNES FOR Te Deum, Jubilate Deo, Magnificat, Nunc Dimittis;

likewise the Order of performing Divine Service by Way of CHANT-
ING, after the Cathedral Manner, suitable for our Country Churches:
With a great Number of PSALMS, HYMNS, and Twenty-three
ANTHEMS, many of them never before published. The THIRD
EDITION, with Additions; the former carefully Corrected and
Amended. By ROBERT BARBER, *Castleton. LONDON:* Printed
by ROBERT BROWN, in *Windmill-Court,* near *Christ's Hospital.*
For CHARLES BATHURST, in *Fleet-Street;* JOSEPH HEATH, at *Not-
tingham* and *Mansfield;* and JOHN ROE, at *Derby.* MDCCLIII.
(octavo; *the* INTRODUCTION, 4 pp.; + 235 pp.; + *A* Table,
1 page.)

AN ALPHABETICAL LIST OF THE *Burgesses* & *Freeholders,* Who POLLED before *John Fellows,* and *Tho. Sands* Gent.
SHERIFFS Of the *Town* and *County* of the *Town* of NOTTING-
HAM, On *Thursday, Friday,* and *Saturday;* the 18th, 19th, and
20th of *April,* M.DCC.LIV. At the ELECTION of Two Burgesses, To represent the said TOWN in *Parliament. Taken in the*
Great Room, *over the* New-Change, *in the* Market-Place; *being
the first Time of its being used for that Purpose. NOTTINGHAM:*
Printed by SAMUEL CRESWELL in the *Market-Place,* and sold by
Mr. Ward Bookseller near the *White-Lion.* M,DCC,LIV. (oct.
58 pp.)

> Lord Howe and Sir Wilughby Aston were elected on this occasion.

* Seasonable Considerations upon the Corn-Trade. With a
short Appendix. By a true born Englishman and Lover of his
Country. London, Printed for, and Sold by H. Cook, at the South
Entrance of the Royal-Exchange and by S. Creswell, Bookseller in
Nottingham, 1757. (oct., 67 pp.)

> If I remember rightly, this book makes favourable mention of Sir
> Charles Sedley.

MEMOIRS OF THE LIFE And GLORIOUS ACTIONS OF
FREDERICK III. KING of *PRUSSIA.* CONTAINING All the
Material Transactions in GERMANY from the Year 1740, to the
End of the Campaign of 1758. In which is included a concise

History of the glorious *Atchievements* of *Prince* FERDINAND of
BRUNSWICK Against the *French* in WESTPHALIA. Published for the
Entertainment and *Improvement* of our BRITISH YOUTH, and proper
to be read at this Juncture by all Lovers of Liberty and their
Country. TO WHICH IS ADDED AN APPENDIX, Containing
a succinct Account of the Person, the Way of Living, and the
Court of the King of *PRUSSIA.* . . . Translated from a curious
Manuscript in FRENCH, found in the Cabinet of the late *Field
Marshal* KEITH. BY W. SALMON, GENT. NOTTINGHAM:
Printed by SAM. CRESWELL, and Sold by J. DEACRES. 1759. (oct.,
112 pp.)

> One of my copies has a portrait of Frederick iii. prefixed; A.
> Pesne Pinx*ᵗ*, G. L. Smith Sculp.

A GENUINE ACCOUNT OF THE LIFE AND TRIAL OF
William Andrew Horne, Esq; Of *Butterley-Hall*, in the County
of *Derby;* Who was convicted at *Nottingham* Assizes, *August* 10,
1759, for the MURDER of a CHILD in the year 1724, and
executed there on the 11th of *December*, 1759. To which is prefixed, A particular Detail of all the Circumstances tending to the
Discovery of this long-conceal'd Murder. *The* SECOND EDI-
TION. *NOTTINGHAM:* Printed by S. CRESWELL, in the *Exchange.* MDCCLIX. [Price Six-Pence.] (oct., 28 pp.)

The Necessity *and* Manner *of being admitted into* Covenant *with*
CHRIST *by* BAPTISM, set forth, *in* A SERMON Preached May 25th,
1760. ON THE Occasion of administring BAPTISM TO ONE of
RIPER YEARS. WITH An ADDRESS to the PEOPLE called
QUAKERS. *By* MATTHEW PILKINGTON, LL.B. Prebendary of
Lichfield. NOTTINGHAM, Printed by SAMUEL CRESWELL in the
New-Change, AND Sold by J. WHISTON and B. WHITE, in *Fleet-
Street, LONDON.* M.D.CC.LX. (oct., 34 pp., + 1 page of ad-
vertisement.)

> The publication of this sermon brought into print, S. Fothergill of
> Warrington and J. Phipps, against it, and E. Owen of Warrington,
> in defence.

A SCHEME For executing A NAVIGATION From Tetney-

Haven to Louth; AND For Draining the low Grounds and Marshes adjoining thereto. By JOHN GRUNDY. TO WHICH IS ADDED THE REPORT OF JOHN SMEATON, Engineer, CONCERNING *The* Practicability &c. *of a* SCHEME *of* Navigation, *from* Tetney *Haven to* Louth, *in the County of* Lincoln, *from a View taken thereof, in* August 1760; *As projected by* Mr. John Grundy *of* Spalding, *Engineer.* NOTTINGHAM: Printed by Samuel Creswell, For E. Parker, Bookseller at *Louth.* MDCCLXI. (oct., title + 24 pp.)

> The last 9 pages are by Smeaton, and dated Austhorpe, July 11, 1761. The Scheme was not carried out; see Smiles's 'Lives of the Engineers,' Vol. II, page 50.

THE PILGRIM'S Progress from This WORLD to That which is to Come; Delivered under the Similitude of a DREAM. In THREE PARTS. Wherein is Discover'd PART I. The *Manner* of his *Setting out;* his dangerous Journey, and safe Arrival at the *Desired Country.* PART II. The Manner of his Setting out of *Christian's* Wife and Children; their dangerous *Journey* and safe *Arrival* at the *Desired Journey.* PART III. The several *Difficulties* and *Dangers* he met with, and the many Victories he obtained over the *World,* the *Flesh* and the *Devil:* Together with his happy Arrival at the Cœlestial City, and the Glory and Joy he found to his Eternal Comfort. By JOHN BUNYAN. *I have used Similitudes.* Hosea XII. 10. The THIRTY-FIRST EDITION, with the Addition of a Number of CUTS. To which is added, The LIFE and DEATH of the AUTHOR. NOTTINGHAM: Printed by S. CRESWELL, *New-Change.* (24mo. small oct. size, 408 pp.)

> This is a cheap reprint. The illustrations are copied and altered from those of 1678, and from those of the 31st edition, printed by A. W. for W. Johnston, London, 1764. Among the errata pointed out to me by Geo. Offor, Esq. are, on the title page, 'The Manner of *his* Setting out,' and 'Desired *Journey;*' page 83, line 28, 'the brute,' is altered to, 'the brewer;' page 223, an answer and question are omitted, and in Joseph's reply, 'state of captivity' is printed instead of 'State of Captivity and Misery;' on page 261 is a duplicate line, 'there is that maketh himself rich, yet hath nothing;' at page 300, line 14, the reading is that of Johnston's ed., second part, page 168,

with the addition of the word 'now.' 'Then the pilgrims got up, and walked to and fro; but how were their eyes now filled with celestial visions! In this land, &c.'

The following descendants of Bunyan were made burgesses of Nottingham at about the date of the above;—George Bunyan, 1752; Wm Bunyan, Lieut^t in the Navy, 1767; Thos Bunyan, hosier, 1776. Of this and of the family at Lincoln I have pedigrees, &c.

A NEW *Introduction* to Learning; OR, A SURE GUIDE To the ENGLISH 𝔓ronunciation and 𝔒rthography: In plain PROSE for the *Ease*, and familiar VERSE for the *Pleasure*, as well as *Profit*, of the Learner. Containing much more on those Subjects than any other Book, in a Method never before attempted; and by which All who can Read may learn, without a Teacher, to Speak and Write *English* as Correctly as they that have had a Liberal Education. Contriv'd so as to amuse and exercise the Ingenious, improve and delight the Less-Knowing, clearly instruct the Ignorant, and allure Youth to a Love of Learning; tho' chiefly design'd for such GROWN Persons as have had but a slender Education, and are desirous of further Improvement. To make it of General Use are added, I. An alphabetical Collection and clear Distinction of above a Thousand Words nearly alike in *Sound*, but different in *Sense* and *Spelling*. II. A large Table of Words, with their Meaning, made *different* in Signification by adding E *Final* III. An Explanation of *Abbreviations*, Notes of *Reference*, and other *Marks* which often occur in Books and Writing. By SAMUEL HAMMOND, Schoolmaster in NOTTINGHAM; *Author of the Complete and Comprehensive* SPELLING-DICTIONARY. NOTTINGHAM: Printed for the *AUTHOR;* By SAMUEL CRESWELL. (16mo., 80 pp.)

This book is very much on the principle of Dr. Sullivan's 'Spelling-book Superseded.'

A Complete and Comprehensive Spelling-Dictionary of the 𝔈nglish 𝔏anguage, on the NEWEST PLAN; For the Use of Young *Gentlemen, Ladies,* and *Others.* Teaching to Spell and Write the Language with great Exactness, by Means of few more than the Primitive Words. So that in Learning to Spell about

5

34 . *Typography of Nottinghamshire.*

Nine Thousand Words many Times the Number will be known with
Certainty, their Dependance on each other shewn, and the Genius
of the Language laid open; by which the Memory will not only be
greatly eas'd and assisted, but much Time and Trouble in attaining
the Language sav'd. The whole being duely accented, to prevent
vicious Pronunciation; the Number of Syllables, in every Word,
fully ascertain'd; and the Part, or Parts, of Speech to which each
Word properly belongs always noted. To which is prefix'd, A
Compendious ENGLISH GRAMMAR; with a HISTORY of the LAN-
GUAGE. MUCH IN LITTLE. *By* SAMUEL HAMMOND; *Schoolmaster in* Nottingham. *Author of the* NEW INTRODUCTION TO
LEARNING, &c. *NOTTINGHAM:* Printed for the Author; by
SAMUEL CRESWELL. (16mo size, partly of 8vo sheets; unpaged,
80 pp.)

POEMS ON VARIOUS SUBJECTS. WHERETO IS PRE-
FIXED A SHORT ESSAY ON THE STRUCTURE OF ENG-
LISH VERSE. By the Rev. LEMUEL ABBOTT. *NOTTING-
HAM:* Printed for the AUTHOR, by SAMUEL CRESWELL.
MDCCLXV. (octavo. Title and dedication, each 1 page; + Sub-
scribers' Names 10 pp.; + Essay 32 pp; + Poems 143 pp.. Title
page partly rubricated.)

A Voyage to North America perform'd by G. Taylor of Sheffield
in the years 1768 and 1769. With an account of his tedious passage of eighteen weeks from Ireland to the American Shore, tho'
there was only six weeks' provision for ninety eight persons. The
extreme hardships the Crew underwent, being under a necessity of
casting lots who should die to satisfy the hunger of the rest. The
Author's Manner of trading with the Indians, a concise History of
their Manners Diversions and barbarous Customs, with his journey
by land from New York to Quebec in Canada, by way of Albany,
Saratoga, Fort Edward, Lake George, Ticonderago, Crown Point,
Lake Champlain, and Moutreal; his Passage from Quebec down
the River St. Lawrence to Boston from the Island Anticosti;
crossing the Gulph to Newfoundland by way of St. John's, Cape
Breton and Halifax; from Boston to Rhode Island and through
the British Settlements, along the Sea Shore to Long Island,
Staten Island through the West and East Jerseys, to Philadelphia:

a particular description of all these places the customs and manners of the inhabitants, and the Manufactures which they carry on. His setting Sail from Philadelphia to New Orleans, in West Florida, up the River Mississippi to the Illinois, and down from Fort Chartres, over the Ohio River, through the Cherokee, Chicsaw, and Chactaw Indian Settlements, to Pensacola ; passing the Gulphs of Mexico and Florida to St. Augustine in East Florida, from thence by Land to Georgia, South Carolina, North Carolina, Virginia, Maryland, and to Philadelphia again ; with a particular account of the Climate, Soil, and Disposition of the Inhabitants in each Settlement, likewise Observations on the Beasts, Birds, Fishes, and other Matters worthy of Notice. The Author's unhappy Shipwreck on the Rock Skillocks to the S.W. of Ireland, within sight of Land, the Ship and Cargo being entirely lost. Nottingham. Printed by S. Creswell for the Author. MDCCLXXI. (Sm. 8vo. Title, + table of contents, 6 pp.; + 248 pp.)

A Letter on the subject of Wool. . . . . . by Wm Mugliston. . . . . . Nottingham : Printed for the Author, by H. Cox . . . . . . 1772. (20 pp.)

AN EXACT LIST OF THE Burgesses and Freeholders, Of the TOWN and COUNTY of the Town of *NOTTINGHAM;* Who POLLED before RALPH NEWHAM, AND WM. HEATH, *Jun.* GENT. SHERIFFS. At the ELECTION of TWO BURGESSES, To serve in PARLIAMENT for the said Town ; Taken on Tuesday, Wednesday, Thursday, and Friday, the 11th, 12th, 13th, and 14th of October 1774. At a BOOTH erected in the *Market Place* for that Purpose, by Adjournment from a Room in the 'Change. Digested into Alphabetical Order, and divided into three distinct Parts, *viz.* I. The *Town Votes.* II. *London Votes.* III. *Country Votes.*— To which is added, a LIST of such VOTES as did not POLL, as far as could be procured. *CANDIDATES.* The Hon. WILLIAM HOWE, of EPPERSTONE ; The Right Hon. EDWARD BENTINCK, Esq ; commonly called LORD EDWARD BENTINCK ; and SIR CHARLES SEDLEY, of NUTTHALL, Bart. *NOTTINGHAM :* Printed by GEORGE BURBAGE, for S. CRESWELL, and G. BURBAGE ; also sold by Mr. WARD, and Mr. HEATH, Booksellers in *Nottingham.* 1774. oct., 72 pp. + errata 2 pp.)

Sedley and Howe were elected.

Samuel Creswell was a tory, (as befitted a grandson of Thomas Hawksley, the Jacobite) and contested the question of the Junior Council against the Whig Corporation; he died Frid. Aug. 25, 1786, from a cold caught on an electioneering expedition to Bestwood Hall. After his death Burbage attempted to deprive his widow of her interest in the Journal. S. C. was the father of Edward Creswell, Vicar of Radford and Lenton, 1803-1840, whose son, Samuel Creswell, is the present Vicar of Radford; also brother of Mrs. Catherine Upton, authoress of Miscellaneous pieces in Prose and Verse, London, 1784, 4to. She accompanied her husband, Lieut. John Upton, of the 72nd or Manchester Regiment, to Gibraltar, and was present at the great siege, on which subject she wrote a poem entitled The Siege of Gibraltar. I have in my possession Lord Heathfield's testimonial to Upton.

Burbage is represented by general tradition as extremely close, not to say worse, in money matters. His dress was after the old fashion and rather imposing, his manners very polite; and the story goes that success once attended a bet, that he would pompously and with many words thank a little girl sent to get from him two halfpence in exchange for a penny.

A Collection of Hymns for the Hearers of the Apostles. Nottingham : Printed for the Society by G. Burbage on the Long Row. M,DCC,LXXVII. (12mo., 402 pp.)

* *The Dying Christian's Triumph* IN A LIVING REDEEMER EXEMPLIFIED IN A SERMON, Preached at SUTTON in ASHFIELD, NOTTINGHAMSHIRE, occasioned by the death of MATTHEW BUTCHER, Jun. who departed this life December 10, 1777, AGED 22 YEARS. By *JOHN BARRETT*. *But why more Woe? more Comfort let it be. Nothing is dead, but that which wish'd to die. Nothing is dead, but Wretchedness and Pain. Nothing is dead, but what encumber'd, gall'd, Block'd up the Pass, and barr'd from real Life.* Young. Printed by A. Bell, No. 8, Aldgate, London; And sold by Joseph Heath, Bookseller, Nottingham and Mansfield. (oct., 48 pp.)

'The Author of the above Sermon, left Sutton in March, 1782, on being chosen to succeed the late Rev. Mr. Fawcett in the Pastoral

Office at Kidderminster, in Worcestershire.' MS. Note in my copy by Mr. Bilby, sometime editor of the Nottingham Journal.

The Gamut· or Scale of Musick. . . . . . . Nottingham Printed & sold by I. Heath Next Door to the Boot & Shoe in the Market Place Bookseller Binder & Stationer. (Single sheet, no date.)

'1789. Jan. 1. Died, Mr. Heath, some years a bookseller in Nottingham. He had been at the Methodist meeting the last night of the year, where he staid till past twelve. On his return home he found Mrs. Heath in bed, and after informing her that the clock had struck twelve, and wishing her many happy new years, he fell back upon the floor and died without a groan.'

The late Mr. Jonathan Dunn bought his business of the executors of Mr. Wilson; who had it from Heath's widow. The purchase was subject to an annuity to Mrs. Heath, who went to reside in Cornwall, and, like most annuitants, made a very long life of it.

THE METHODIST: ATTEMPTED IN PLAIN METRE. *Laudatur ab his, culpatur ab illis.* Hor. *Sempiterno nominabitur. Noli putare me hæc auribus tuis dare.* NOTTINGHAM: *PRINTED for the AUTHOR,* At G. BURBAGE'S Office on the Long-Row. M,DCC,LXXX. (square oct., 134 pp.)

This work, which is a kind of epic, is supposed to have been written by J. Kershaw, a Wesleyan minister.

POEMS ON VARIOUS SUBJECTS, DIVINE and MORAL. By A. GOODRICK. —— "if vain our Toil, We ought to blame the Culture, not the Soil." POPE. NOTTINGHAM: PRINTED for the AUTHOR, And SOLD by G. BURBAGE, on the LONG-ROW; and J. OSCROFT, MANSFIELD. M,DCC,LXXX. Price TWO SHILLINGS. (Quarto, 68 pp.)

Dated Sutton in Ashfield, *March* 1, 1780.

CONCISE ESSAYS UPON VARIOUS PHILOSOPHICAL AND CHEMICAL SUBJECTS; Proper to be Read before or

AFTER ATTENDING COURSES OF CHEMISTRY, OR, EXPERIMENTAL PHILOSOPHY: *UNDER THE FOLLOWING HEADS,* VIZ. MATTER *and* MOTION, CHEMICAL PRINCIPLES *and* PROCESSES, USEFUL TABLES, AND A VOCABULARY. By J. WARLTIRE. NOTTINGHAM: PRINTED BY H. Cox. M DCC LXXXI. (oct., 70 pp.)

A Contemplative Walk with the Author's Wife and Children. . . . . . . by William Mugliston. . . . . . . Nottingham : Printed for the Author, by Henry Cox, 1782. . . . . .

THE PATRIOT SOLDIER; A POEM.—Οὗ οἱ ἀεικὲς ἀμυνομένῳ περὶ πάτρης Τεθνάμεν· ἀλλ' ἄλοχός τε σόη καὶ παῖδες ὀπίσσω, καὶ οἶκος, καὶ κλῆρος ἀκήρατος. Hom. Il. B. XV. *And for our country 'tis a bliss to die. The gallant man tho' slain in fight he be, Yet leaves his nation safe, his children free ; Entails a debt on all the grateful state ; His own brave friends shall glory in his fate ; His wife lives honour'd, all his race succeed ; And late posterity enjoy the deed!* Pope's transl. By JOHN EDWARDS, Esq. MAJOR *of* LIGHT DRAGOONS *in the* VOLUNTEER ARMY *of* IRELAND. NOTTINGHAM : PRINTED BY SAMUEL TUPMAN, BOOKSELLER ; AND SOLD BY T. LONGMAN, PATER-NOSTER-ROW, AND T. AND W. LOWNDES, FLEET-STREET, LONDON. M DCC LXXXIV. (oct., quarto size. Title and dedication, each 1 page ; + Advertisement, 2 pp.; + The Argument, 1 page ; + 35 pp.)

> Dated from *OLD COURT, July the First,* 1784. I have corrected the printer's Greek.

A NARRATIVE OF WHAT PASSED AT THE REVOLUTION HOUSE, AT WHITTINGTON, COUNTY OF DERBY, IN THE YEAR 1688. WITH A PERSPECTIVE VIEW, AND PLAN OF THAT COTTAGE. NOTTINGHAM ; PRINTED BY SAMUEL TUPMAN. (Quarto, 11 pp. + plate.)

> For distribution among Major Rooke's friends : the Narrative by the learned Dr. Pegge, then Rector of Whittington ; the View and Plan, drawn by Rooke, engraved by Basire.

REMARKS ON THE COINAGE OF *ENGLAND* FROM
THE EARLIEST TO THE PRESENT TIMES; WITH A
VIEW TO POINT OUT THE CAUSES OF THE PRESENT
SCARCITY OF SILVER FOR CHANGE, AND TO SHEW
THE ONLY PROPER WAY TO MAKE IT PLENTIFUL.
TO WHICH IS ADDED An APPENDIX, CONTAINING
OBSERVATIONS UPON THE ANCIENT ROMAN COIN-
AGE; AND A DESCRIPTION OF SOME MEDALS AND
COINS FOUND NEAR *NOTTINGHAM.* By WALTER
MERREY. NOTTINGHAM: Printed by S. TUPMAN, AND
SOLD BY T. LONGMAN, PATER-NOSTER-ROW, LONDON.
MDCCLXXXIX. (oct., 108 pp.)

> Tupman's business descended thus; Tupman, Barnett, Stavely.
> Merrey was a Scotchman, and Creswell's former assistant and friend.

THE GRAVE. A POEM, BY *ROBERT BLAIR.* *The House
appointed for all living.* Job. NOTTINGHAM: Printed for
W. Gray, opposite the Hen-Cross. M,DCC,LXXXIX. (12mo.,
21 pp.; also printed with it, but paged separately are the following,)

AN ELEGY WRITTEN IN A COUNTRY CHURCH-YARD.
BY Mr. GRAY. NOTTINGHAM: Printed for W. Gray, opposite the Hen-Cross. M,DCC,LXXXIX. (6 pp.)

A NIGHT-PIECE ON DEATH. (3 pp.)

> The excitement caused by the French Revolution of this year
> brought to light many ephemeral productions, of which I have no
> sufficient knowledge; about the same time the character of the purely
> local books declined. Hence it is thought better to defer this new
> class of literature to a future occasion.

INDEX OF PERSONS.

N.B.—The figures in *brackets* attached to a name, denote the number of times it occurs on the page indicated.

A. W., 32.
Abbott, Rev. Lemuel, 34.
Abney, 18.
Allestree, H., 12(²), 14, 16(²), 22.
Alwood, Mr. John, 26.
Angelo, Dr. Nathanael, 8.
Ann, Queen, 12(²).
Aston, Sir Wilughby, 30.
Ayscough, Wm., 10(²), 11(²), 13(7), 14(²), 16(³), 17, 18, 19(²).
———— Anne, 13(²), 20, 21(²), 23, 25.
———— George, 23(³), 27(²), 28(²), 29(⁵).
———— Rev. Samuel, F.S.A., 29.

Bainbrigge, Thomas, 11.
Bangor, Bp. of, 8.
Barber, Robert, Castleton, 30.
Bargrave, Isaac and Elizabeth, 13.
Barker, E. H., 19.
Barnett, 39.
Barrett, Rev. John, M.A., 6(³), 7, 9, 10(³), 11.
——— Joseph, 6, 26.
——— John, 36.
Basire, 38.
Bateson, Mr. Richard, 24, 25(²), 27.
Bathurst, Charles, 30.
Bell, A., 36.
Bentinck, Lord Edward, 35.
Bentley, 16, 17—18, 19(²).
Berdmore, Samuel, 7, 15(²).
Bilby, Mr., 37.
Blair, Robert, 39.
Booth, Mr. Peniston, 19(³).

Bourn, 22, 24.
Bradley, J., 22.
Brailsford, Rev. John, A.M., 27(²).
Bramhall, Abp., 10.
Brown, Robert, 30.
Brunswick, Prince Ferdinand of, 31.
Bunyan, John, 32, 33.
——— George, William, and Thomas, 33.
Burbage, George, 28, 35, 36(³), 37(²).
Burnet, Bp., 9.
Butcher, Matthew, Jun., 36.

Cantrel, H., 22.
Cantrell, Henry, M.A., 11(⁴), 12(³).
Carpenter, 11.
Chadwick, Daniel, 6.
Charles I., 11(²).
Cheshire, John, M.B., 29.
Churchill, Awnsham, 6.
Clarke, Edward, 7.
Clay, John, 20(²).
Clegg, J., V.D.M., M.D., 26.
Clements, Henry, 18.
Cliff, N., 9, 10.
Collyer, J., 8, 9(³), 10(²), 11, 12(²), 14 ², 15(³), 20(²), 22(³), 26.
——— Tho., 23, 24, 26, 27, 28(⁴).
Comyns, Mr. Baron, 24.
Cook, H., 30.
Cotton, Charles, 22, 28.
Cox, H., 35, 38(²).
Creswell, Samuel, 28, 30(²), 31(³), 32(²), 33, 34(²), 35(²), 36(²), 39.

INDEX OF SUBJECTS.

LONDON:
PRINTED BY FREDERICK PICKTON,
89, GREAT PORTLAND STREET, OXFORD STREET.

www.ingramcontent.com/pod-product-compliance
Lightning Source LLC
Chambersburg PA
CBHW021439090426
42739CB00009B/1549